"Regular family meditation sessions have allowed us to slow down and be together in a grounded way that's free of conflict and tension. There is a feeling of spaciousness and unity that makes our hectic lives more manageable."

-Lisa Cargerman, PhD
Child psychologist, wife and mother of three

"I'm a single parent with a small company to run, shifts to fill, and deadlines to meet, and even though meditation sometimes looks like one more thing I don't need to add to my stressful life, I find myself making the time anyway. Those few minutes of sitting together are like an oasis. It's a peaceful time for us to be quietly joyful with each other, and somehow it makes all our rushing around not be so *rushed*. When we don't meditate, there's a noticeable level of irritability – we end up snapping at each other a lot more."

-Amy Kida
Single mother of two school-aged children

D1599215

"My 12 year-old son and I started sitting together at the beginning of the school year. Why? I had observed in him some growing pangs and poor choices in the passage to middle school. Although an accomplished musician and martial artist, at times he could be willful and unkind. I feared that if we followed the typical father/son dynamic, our lifelong friendship might be at risk of breaking down in the stormy days of adolescence that lie ahead. So now we meditate every day for 10 minutes, just before he leaves for school. Sitting together in silence, following our breath, there is a sense that time has paused for a moment. Unplugged from the speedy pace of life, and from alpha male struggles, we find ourselves re-connecting to our mutual love and respect. There is a message in it for both of us. Life can be hard, but you're not in this alone."

-John Crowe, MSW

Social worker and father of two

◎◎◎

Kerry Lee MacLean has been practicing meditation for thirty years with renowned meditation masters Chogyam Trungpa and Sakyong Mipham. She received her BA in Contemplative Psychology from Naropa University and has directed the Colorado Shambhala Children's Rites of Passage Meditative Arts courses for nine years. She is the author of seven children's picture books, including *Peaceful Piggy Meditation* and has been teaching child and family meditation programs for over sixteen years. She is the happy mother of five very decent human beings.

Also by Kerry Lee MacLean

Peaceful Piggy Meditation
Pigs Over Shambhala
Pigs Over Boulder
Pigs Over Denver
Pigs Over Colorado
Pigs Over Colorado Past
Sophie's Not Afraid!

All are available at www . ziji . com

This book distributed by New Leaf
Children's books distributed by Books West
303-449-5995

The Family Meditation Book

How practicing being peaceful together for ten minutes
a day can make life saner
(and more pleasant)
for even the busiest families.

Kerry Lee MacLean

On the Spot! Books

On the Spot! Books
1492 Tipperary Street
Boulder, CO 80303
Onthespotbooks@msn.com

Copyright 2004 Kerry Lee MacLean
Cover artwork by Kerry Lee MacLean

All rights reserved. This book, or parts thereof, may not
be reproduced in any form without permission,
excepting brief quotes used in connection with reviews.

ISBN   0-9652998-6-4
LCCN   2004093296

First Printing

Printed in Hong Kong by Sunrise Design and Printing

To my meditation teachers

Chogyam Trungpa, Rinpoche
and
Sakyong Mipham, Rinpoche

ACKNOWLEDGEMENTS

I am most grateful to Chogyam Trungpa and Sakyong Mipham for showing me how to tame my wild and crazy mind, turning it into an ally.

If it weren't for my wonderful husband and children meditating with me for the past twelve years, this book wouldn't, *couldn't* have been written. Thanks for meditating with me.

Special thanks to Judith Simmer-Brown, PhD, whose insight helped clarify the vision of this book.

Hector MacLean, Kelly MacLean, Tessa Maclaren, Amy Kida and Leland Williams gave great encouragement, insight and practical help.

CONTENTS

◎ ◎ ◎

Part I
Family Meditation Sessions
How, Why, Where and When to Meditate Together

◎◎◎

Part II
The Six Strengths
How Meditation Improves Family Relationships

◎◎◎

�☉☉

FOREWORD

"Like sleeping or eating, meditation brings health and happiness. It gives us all -- including our children -- the opportunity to bring peace to ourselves and to our families. A family that has peace has everything. Kerry Lee MacLean's book is a wonderful resource for learning to be together in peace and happiness."

—Sakyong Mipham, author of
Turning the Mind into an Ally

Part I

Family Meditation Sessions

How, Why, Where and When to Meditate Together

◎

Chapter One

The Many Benefits of Meditating with Your Children (and the science to back it up)

In this busy, crazy world, it's good to have a peaceful place inside. What a refreshing idea – to stop and practice being peaceful together for a few minutes each day. If you think about it, it's a revolutionary idea. Who ever heard of a family stopping to do nothing? To simply be together. Of course, the neighbors might think we're *mad.* But in truth, we're no longer just paying lip service to world peace; we're cultivating peace right where it truly begins, in our homes, in our hearts and minds.

In an era when families can barely find the time to sit down and enjoy their meals together, brief meditation sessions create a precious opportunity for family togetherness. And let's face it, in this high-tech, high-speed, high-stress society, where even our children are always on the go, where violent images surround us, where words like 'terrorism' and 'war' are a part of everyday conversation, where astonishing numbers of us are taking medication for depression and anxiety; and worse, where thousands of parents are desperately giving these same drugs to their children for emotional and behavioral problems, in such a world, it's more important than ever to take the time as a family to create and maintain a peaceful place inside ourselves.

As parents of five children, ages 17 to 25 (two his, two mine, and one ours) my husband, Hector, and I discovered that the simple act of abiding peacefully together for ten minutes each day helps us and our children to:

- De-stress
- Soothe emotional turmoil
- Calm anxiety
- Settle nervous energy
- Increase self-esteem
- Arouse confidence
- Face fears

- Enhance the ability to self-reflect
- Deepen concentration
- Arouse natural empathy
- Open channels of communication between all family members
- Foster family bonding
- Build and strengthen inner peace

How? Regular meditation clears that cloud of confusion that gathers in our minds as a result of rushing around all the time and not working through and letting go of old hurts and disappointments – in short, the emotional baggage of our lives. This dark cloud is the root cause of:

- Anger
- Resentment
- Depression
- Anxiety
- Fearfulness
- Emotional turmoil
- Low self-esteem
- Impatience

- Restlessness
- Speediness
- Insensitivity
- Lack of empathy
- Inability to concentrate
- Inability to self-reflect
- Negative, whiney attitudes

Can meditation really help with all that? Yes and it's been proven![1] The past thirty years of research by top doctors and neuroscientists have produced extraordinary and very exciting data about how meditation calms and feeds the body, mind and spirit, making life saner and more enjoyable for those who practice it regularly. Of course, this is old news in the East. They've known the benefits of meditation for thousands of years. And now, thanks to ivy league educated research doctors who discovered meditation in the early 1970's, such practical wisdom is finally being

---

[1] Read Dr. Daniel Goleman's <u>newly updated</u> version of *Destructive Emotions, A Scientific Dialogue with the Dalai Lama* and *Meditation for Optimum Health* by Andrew Weil, Md and Jon Kabat-Zinn, Phd.

validated and accepted into mainstream western medicine.

Using the very latest in EEG and MRI technology, researchers have discovered that even beginning meditators will experience *significantly* better moods, less stress and anxiety, lower blood pressure, a stronger immune system, relief from chronic pain and accelerated healing of a whole score of diseases. The benefits are seemingly endless.

According to recent studies by a high level neurology and brain psychology team working with the Dalai Lama and his monks, the latest research (see last footnote) proves that meditation deactivates the right prefrontal lobe, which produces negative feelings like sadness, anxiety and worry. At the same time, it activates the *left* prefrontal lobe, responsible for positive feelings such as happiness, enthusiasm, joy, high energy and alertness. Anyone familiar with the Dalai Lama's joyfully energetic presence has seen this truth demonstrated in abundance!

If you stop and think about it, we westerners have never had clearly defined tools for working with our mind and emotions. When we were kids, our parents might have said "cheer up" or "calm down", or at best, "you need to go for a walk and cool off", but that was really about it. No one ever said, "sit down and use this technique to relax your mind for a few minutes every day. It will prevent you from getting overly depressed or riled up about things." I certainly never had that. Now that we have access to such helpful tools, let's put them to good use!

As for our blended family of seven, we found that regular meditation sessions (beginning about twelve years ago) began to work wonders. Not only did each individual family member slow down and cheer up, but the entire family dynamic began to change in ways we never expected. New channels of communication opened up that we didn't even realize were missing. After awhile we found ourselves on a whole new ground, a much more open, loving, supportive and enriching one than we stood on before.

This book is my attempt to share our fortunate discovery with families struggling to create health and harmony at home in a world that's getting crazier all the time.

Think of Meditation as Daily Exercise

Here in the West, we tend to think of meditation as some strange, mysterious activity, but in much of the world, meditation is simply an ordinary and necessary part of the everyday self-care routine. The popular view is that you have to eat right, get enough sleep and exercise both your body and your mind in order to have a good day. It's as simple as that. Meditation is just mental jogging to them. And, like jogging, if you haven't done it in a while, or if you've *never* done it, it's going to be a bit of a challenge at first. But once your meditation muscles are in shape, it actually feels good and wholesome to meditate for ten minutes, in much the same way that going for an early morning run feels fantastic to the seasoned jogger.

A Still-Point Inside

As a lifelong meditator and city-dweller, I've noticed that people who meditate regularly smile more often than people who don't. They're more pleasant to be around. They're more relaxed and cheerful than most of the people around them.

Meditation awakens clarity and deepens mental/emotional relaxation, giving both parents and their children an invaluable still-point inside. Family members can check in with this peaceful still-point at any time in any situation, enabling them to make better choices about the things that really count, making the difference between unintentionally causing harm, and doing the right thing.

If you think about it, anyone and everyone can benefit from developing that peaceful place inside themselves, regardless of age, race or religion. And they'll benefit on many different levels, with greater physical, mental, and emotional health all around.

@

Chapter Two

Our Story

*How seven busy people learned to live
in harmony under one roof*

I don't want to give the wrong impression here.
Hector and I didn't start out as incredibly enlightened
parents who, in spite of having five kids and two
businesses to run, spontaneously realized the value of
meditating with our children. The truth is, although we
ourselves had been meditating since we were teenagers,
we had no intention of including our children in our
private meditation sessions. We feared it might be
'laying our trip' on them. We figured they'd get into
meditation later in their lives, if they wanted to. Not
until we'd all been living together awhile and began to
suspect that we weren't going to automatically blend
into one, big happy step-family did we start looking

around for ways to help our children cope with some pretty complicated relationships.

Our kids were dealing with the usual emotional baggage that goes along with blending step-families together: power struggles, questions of holding back love in loyalty to the other parents, questions of belonging or *not belonging*. Not to mention radically different codes of discipline between households – enough to make anyone feel schizophrenic - *and act schizophrenic!* Eventually, things escalated to the point where we felt we were in a full-scale crisis. We weren't sure this blended family was even going to make it. The word 'divorce' came up all too often.

Meditation was the only thing that helped my husband and I to navigate those murky waters. And at some point it began to dawn on us that if meditation helped *us* cope with such overwhelming emotions, by making us slow down and communicate better with each other, maybe it would help our children, too.

So, it was only out of desperation that we instituted our daily family meditation sessions. All five kids complained at first but soon got used to it and believe it or not, most of them even came to *like it*. After

only a year or two we found that not only had we
survived the crisis, we were actually thriving. Our
family was very much on the way to becoming the close
knit clan we were working towards.

Before long, we decided not to make the
meditation sessions mandatory anymore, because we
still weren't very comfortable with 'forcing' our kids to
meditate. All five children chose to stop sitting, though,
interestingly, they still dropped in on our sessions
occasionally. Nonetheless, within two weeks Hector
and I had both noticed how family communication on
every level was deteriorating. The kids seemed a tad
speedier, more self-centered, a little less prone to self
reflect or empathize with each other. In other words,
they were grumpier, whinier, more selfish, and meaner!
That's when we realized that our family meditation
sessions were responsible for much of the peace and
harmony we'd been enjoying. Daily sitting sessions had
been silently improving the way our kids related with
each other. They had become more tolerant of each
other, more sensitive – or it might be more accurate to
say more *perceptive* of each other, thereby increasing

their emotional intelligence. In short, meditation helped turn our children into more responsive and reasonable people. Once we realized what was going on, we looked at each other and said, "Let's reinstate the family meditation sessions immediately!"

We called a family meeting. "Look," Hector told them, "you were a lot happier when you were sitting every day. We want you to come back to meditating with us in our morning sessions."

"Think of it this way," I added. "You have to brush and floss your teeth every day to keep them clean and healthy, and you have to sit every day to keep your minds happy and healthy. You take good care of your bodies, you take good care of your minds." Most of them didn't even bother to argue. They *knew* everyone had been getting along better when they'd been sitting with us every morning and they didn't like the way things were going either. In a house of seven people (with *one* bathroom) it hadn't taken long for the subtle shift in mood to put us all on edge.

Though we never quite got back to the discipline of sitting together every single day, we did manage it three or four times a week. Now that we're down to two kids in the house, one in college and one graduating high school, we sometimes only manage two or three times a week. But it's still working. Perhaps we're taking advantage of the cumulative effect of so many years of meditation. In any case, I feel so fortunate to be able to say that our children are some of the most amiable, confident, poised, and good-humored young people I know. Friends in our community come up to me often asking how they turned out to be so confident, warm, and cheerful. The only thing I can think to say is, "We've been meditating together a long time. It seems to make them happy."

◎

Chapter Three

Creating A Sacred Space
How to set up a meditation area

The first step in meditating together is finding a good place for your family meditation sessions. It could be just an out-of-the-way, quiet corner somewhere or (if you can) use a whole room. Imagine having an entire room dedicated to cultivating peace within your family. Now that makes a strong statement to your children – and yourselves for that matter. At our house, it was packed to the gills; and there was constant chaos with two home-based businesses and five kids. So we put our shrine in our bedroom. It's a large converted garage where there's enough room for all seven of us to sit, on the rare occasion we're all at home together.

So, what is a sacred space? A sacred space is an environment that wakes you up and reminds you of the sacredness of life. Obviously, the opposite of a sacred space would be cluttered and dirty, dark and dank, people might be coming through all the time, it might be noisy and chaotic. Such a place could be depressing. On the other hand, if you created a space that was clean, light and spacious, quiet, visually uplifting and out of the way of traffic, it might have the opposite effect. It might lift depression, calm anxiety, and invite your family to slow down and appreciate their world by awakening their five senses, instead of feeling they have to shut down to keep the chaos out. And heightened senses naturally see and appreciate the beauty in life that frazzled senses often miss: the delicacy of a flower, the way raindrops race each other down a windowpane, the sound of crickets chirping in the night.

The Shrine

You should set up your shrine according to your own spiritual beliefs or religion, but here are some general guidelines you can use if you like. You can find most of these items in your local gift store, or order through a catalog.[2]

Shrine Table

An elevated shrine is good for keeping the burning incense and candles out of young children's curious little fingers. Putting a shrine up high can also be a way of showing respect. Ours is a three-foot high wooden box, covered with batting, then satin. We have a sheet of glass on top to protect the silk from wax drippings. Of course, you can use any small table that seems suitable for the space you're working with.

You can cover your shrine table with beautiful silks and brocades, or any nice cloth. In keeping with creating a sacred space, you might want to be careful not to clutter the shrine with lots of objects. Keep it simple but elegant.

---

[2] Order through www . ziji . com. I don't get a commission, but they are good friends with high quality meditation supplies.

Central Object

The central object should be something that truly has the power to stop your rushing mind, even if it's just for an instant. You might choose a crystal ball, which represents the clarity of a settled mind. A statue of the Buddha sitting serenely in meditation is always a good choice, because it's a perfect visual reminder of what we're trying to accomplish in our meditation sessions, to create and maintain a serene and peaceful place inside ourselves.

Incense and Burner

Incense burns at a calm and steady pace, again, the perfect reminder of why we're sitting there in the first place. Incense has a natural elegance. Our family prefers Japanese incense, but there are all kinds (Tibetan, Japanese and Indian are easy to find) and there are different beliefs as to its significance. Some say incense symbolizes patience and equanimity, like the slow steady walk of an elephant. Several eastern cultures believe the perfumed white smoke attracts the blessings and wisdom of our unseen protectors – our ancestors, the relatives, teachers, loved ones and protectors who have gone before us.

It's wonderful if your spouse or one of the children gets to choose the type of incense, or the incense burner, so that they feel they helped to create this space, too. Participation in creating the sacred space is important for the whole family, so that they take pride in helping to create this uplifted and extraordinary area in their home, too.

Candles

As with the incense, it's nice if one of the children gets to pick out the candles and candle holders. Some people have just one candle, others use two, placing one on either side of the central object.

Flowers

A vase with nicely arranged fresh or silk flowers uplifts your shrine, making it visually pleasing and somehow special. Again, it's good if a spouse or child gets to pick these out or helps with the arrangement.

Fresh flowers in particular can remind us of the freshness and impermanence of the present moment.

They can also symbolize an open heart – loving-kindness and genuine compassion.

Gong

Gongs, with their extraordinary reverberating sound, are perfect for helping the mind transition in and out of meditation. They also mark the time and space, beginning and ending your session with clarity. If you don't have one, you can always use a bell or even a metal mixing bowl (struck hard with a pencil eraser). If you do have a gong, encourage everyone to sit still, listening to the ever-widening circles of sound radiating out at the end of your meditation session. Refrain from moving or speaking until the sound has completely dissipated, so that you can relax in the space you've created.

Pictures

Near the shrine you can hang pictures on the wall of your spiritual guides, whomever your spiritual teachers may be – the Dalai Lama, Christ, Buddha, Dr. Martin Luther King, Jr., – or someone you know personally – pretty much *anyone* who inspires you to work at becoming a wiser and more peaceful person.

Meditation Cushion

It's important for every family member to have his or her very own cushion – right down to the youngest child. Our friends at ziji.com are now carrying children's meditation cushions in a smaller size and in fun fabrics that kids will love. I recommend using a zafu, which is a round, slightly flat cushion; but if you're tall, you might be more comfortable with a gomden, which has more height and is rectangular. Some gift shops are carrying beautiful silk brocade zafus, with buckwheat hulls for filling. Or, you can just use the pillows from your couch. If you're sitting on a wood floor, you might want to use a folded blanket underneath or buy a zabuton, the large pad that goes with meditation cushions. A yoga mat will do nicely, too.

Setting it all up

If possible, make the setting up of the shrine a family project. Believe it or not, these little rituals will

pique everyone's curiosity and make even the most
restless person look forward to the meditation session.

◎

Chapter Four
The Family Meditation Session
The Art of Abiding Peacefully Together

Including Young Children

Young children will benefit just as much from being a part of the family meditation session as everyone else, but it's important to keep in mind that it's not realistic to expect young ones to sit perfectly still for ten minutes at a time. And I wouldn't recommend teaching the breathing technique to kids under eight or nine, either.

Still, they'll get more out of the family sessions than you might expect. First of all, just knowing they have their very own meditation cushion saved for them in the families' sacred space means so much to them. Children are very sensitive. The psychological impact of watching the way their parents and older siblings behave in the family sacred space is profound, and it prepares them for beginning to learn how to stop, abandon any aggressive tendencies and cultivate peacefulness, too. That may sound like a tall order for one so young, but the truth is meditation often comes more easily to a child's open mind, than to an adults.

It's completely normal for younger kids to come in and squirm around a bit, trying to be quiet for a few minutes at a time while everyone else sits still, following their breath. Maybe they'll sit on their own cushion, or lay quietly with their head on mom or dad's lap for awhile, then go get a book and come back in and read for a bit. That's a very powerful beginning for them. Just learning to be silent and still is a very big deal for young children, particularly in our culture. And in the meantime, they're soaking up the peaceful atmosphere through their very pores, as children do. Over the years they'll get better and better at practicing being peaceful, and one day they may surprise you by deciding to sit with perfect posture the whole ten minutes! It happened with our most restless child when she was only five, so it can happen to *anyone*.

Two days ago, that same daughter, now seventeen, woke me up from my sickbed to meditate with her. "No, I'm too sick," I whined.

"Well, it always makes me feel better when I'm sick," she said. What kind of a ruthless person have I raised, I wondered as she dragged me across the room by the hand. Fifteen minutes later she rang the gong to end our meditation, and I couldn't believe how much lighter I felt. She was right. My throat still hurt, but suddenly my world didn't look quite so bleak.

Amazingly, all of our children have grown into young adults who appreciate the value of meditation, and most of them actually practice it on their own regularly.

Including Teenagers

Teenagers will probably be more inspired to try meditation if you present it as a self-care regimen - they *know* from their own personal experiences and from watching other kids at school just how painful emotions can get. Teenagers will also appreciate your point of view if you present meditation as an exercise in getting to know themselves. They're very interested in exploring who they are, what their beliefs are and how they feel about the big issues in life, and meditation is probably the most powerful way to go about it. In the history of mankind, a better way to 'know thyself' has not been taught.

Be sure to try the Mind-in-a-Jar Experiment (below) with your teenagers because they'll really be able to relate to it.

You might be surprised at how enthusiastic teenagers can be about starting a teen meditation group (perhaps through their school or their spiritual community). My daughter, Sophie, is running one right now, and it's very popular. And, my son, Andrew, just attended a nationwide conference on setting up summer meditation camps for children and teenagers[3] worldwide.

So many of our teenagers are thirsty and hungry for a sense of authentic spirituality in their lives. They're ready to connect with their innermost selves. They long to connect with each other. They need to be a part of

---

[3] See Shambhala Sun Camp in the Resource section.

something bigger than themselves. Teen meditation groups might be the perfect place to meet those needs.

Finding the Right Time

Morning is the perfect time to enjoy meditation, when the energy of the world is naturally awakening and arising, and when your mind is fresh and clear and ready for another day. So, it's great if you can get into the habit of setting the alarm clock fifteen minutes, or even a half hour earlier than usual, which will give plenty of time to wake up peacefully together in your sacred space. It's especially nice if you can make herbal tea or coffee or even hot chocolate for everyone to enjoy at the end of your meditation session together. Some of our most treasured memories come from moments like this. What a rare and wonderful experience, to sit serenely sipping your morning coffee with your spouse and children, while the whole family is in a fresh, yet peaceful, state of mind. That's something every parent should experience at least once in their lives! Possibly even every day! Why not?

After school is another natural break time for everyone to stop and practice being peaceful together.

It's the perfect time to hear about everyone's day, too. What a fantastic opportunity for children especially, to talk about, process and let go of any concerns from their six hours at school – and believe me, they'll have them. It's the perfect way for you to keep your finger on the pulse of every child.

Some parents find they can only pull everyone together at the end of the day, just before bedtime, which makes for a very pleasant way to end the day and prepare everyone to enter sleep in a clear and serene state of mind.

Making Personal Meditation Time

Parents who've been meditating for years might want to meditate longer that ten or fifteen minutes. We deal with this either by simply staying and meditating longer after the rest of the family has left or by doing longer sessions on weekends. When our kids were younger, we used to take turns with long practice sessions while the other parent cared for the children. If you have friends who have children and meditate, too, you can take turns, either one on one or in small groups, trading places half way through your time together.

There are similar small groups residing peacefully together across the United States, Canada, Great Britain, Ireland, Europe, Australia, New Zealand and most recently, South America[4].

Before Meditation

If there's time, yoga stretches are a pleasant way to relax and energize body and mind before meditation. Again, you can set the mood for family meditation sessions by getting into the habit of making a nice cup of herbal tea, coffee or hot chocolate for everyone. Bring it into your meditation area to enjoy together after the session ends when everyone's feeling peaceful, and before you all have to dash off in ten different directions! These little touches help turn your sessions into something warm and wonderful that everyone looks forward to.

Shrine Room Etiquette

The sacred space or shrine room is the one place where no aggression, not even the subtlest form of

---

[4] See resources for a group near you.

passive aggressive behavior, should be tolerated. Everyone should be expected to be on his or her best behavior. Harsh words on the part of parents or children should simply not be allowed. Good discipline in this case is a kindness to everyone.

If you like, everyone can bow on entering and leaving the sacred space. This helps to keep the sacred space sacred, especially if it's in the living room or some place people use for other activities during the normal course of the day.

Bowing should not be a somber, heavy, big deal. Just putting the hands together and bowing slightly is enough to maintain the sense of sacredness. Bowing signals that we are entering a sacred space and helps to uplift everyone's spirits.

Mind-in-a-Jar Experiment

You might find this activity helpful before the first session. Before meditating, fill a glass jar with water. Everyone take a good look at it. Then say something like, "This is your mind – naturally clean, light and clear." Now scoop up a little soil, from outside. Make sure there are no bits of dead grass or plant matter mixed in. Think about letting everyone take turns putting a pinch at a time into the jar. Say something like, "Each tiny grain of this soil is one of our thoughts. Some are happy thoughts, some are sad, some are exciting wishes, some are dark and angry feelings." Put a lid on the jar and swirl it around, so the water and soil swirl around faster and faster. Say, "This is your mind in a hurry."

Now, let everything calm down by letting the jar sit still on a table and say, "This is your mind during meditation. Watch the thoughts settle down to the bottom, leaving the water - our minds – the way they were in the first place, not heavy, dark and muddy, but clear, light and clean. Now we can act peacefully, because we can think clearly!"

Just for fun, place the jar on a nearby shelf or windowsill and you can all check in on it before or after sitting over the next few days. How long did it take for the water to *completely* clear up?

Getting Started

It's nice if you can have a child help you light the candle and incense. Then, if you're inspired, you can bow to the shrine together. Again, the bow is just a light, gentle acknowledgement of the sacred wakefulness of the space.

Posture

Sit like cross-legged, like the Buddha. Having good posture is important for creating an uplifted state of mind. For contrast, have everyone slouch heavily and notice how restricted breathing and slumped postures can actually make you feel heavy and depressed. Now take your posture again, with good head and shoulders. Rest your relaxed and unfocused eyes a few feet ahead of you (three or four for adults, two or three for children). Keep your back straight, but not rigid. Take your seat with the excellent and regal posture of a king or queen, feeling the strength of the solid earth beneath you, the vast sky above you, and your own personal dignity as a human being bridging them together, joining heaven and earth.

Ring the Gong to Start

Ring the gong once to begin your meditation session and place the striker on the ground, listening to the sound reverberating out. It's nice if your children get to take turns ringing the gong to start, and then a parent can ring the gong to end, so the child doesn't become obsessed with the clock the whole time. Or, you can always just set a silent timer so you don't have to worry about watching the clock. But then you would lose the wonderful quality of the gong's sound echoing out through time and space.

Settling In

When we first sit down, it's a good idea to just settle in for a minute, before we begin practicing the technique. It helps to take the time to feel 'who you are' at that particular moment in time. The natural speed with which we operate is such that when we first stop we spin and spin around in our thoughts – very much like Wile E. Coyote in the Roadrunner cartoons. He runs so fast his head goes 'b-o-o-i-i-ng-ng-ng', back and forth for several seconds after he stops. That's us when we first sit down. B-o-o-i-i-ng-ng-ng. Our thoughts bounce back and forth, back and forth, without much sense, really.

So we need to take the time to settle down and become present with ourselves. Then we can feel clearly 'who we are' at that particular moment. Maybe we're in a rotten mood, maybe we're depressed. Maybe we'll find ourselves in an exceptionally good mood, or we might be scattered, running around in circles of thought. Or, we could feel nothing... - just *flat*. Whatever the case, it doesn't matter, we just need to take stock and acknowledge what state of mind we're beginning our meditation with. That way we can have some idea of what to work toward in our session.

If we're tired and our grumpy, we shouldn't expect to have perfect form and discipline in working with our thoughts, which may be fuzzier than usual. But if we got enough rest and had an excellent breakfast and the sun is shining that day, we might be able to go further and deeper with our meditation than usual.

State Your Plan

It's important to begin with a clearly stated plan, so that you don't end up spacing out the whole ten minutes, wandering in your thoughts. So, when you're ready to begin the technique you can say something like, "Just for the next ten minutes I'm going to train my mind to my breath. The other 1,425 minutes in my day I can follow my thoughts down any interesting, exciting, happy or horrifying trail they want to wander down. But for just this short time I'm going to let go of my thoughts and be fully present here in this room with my breath."

How Long Should We Meditate?

Ten minutes is good for a daily family practice, and if you can stick with that you'll be very happy with the results. On weekends when you have more time and if your children are older, it might be nice to sit for fifteen or twenty minutes. The longer you sit, the more settled you all become. Some of my friends sit for forty-five minutes or even an hour every single day, and they are very dedicated to their discipline.

Once you've become comfortable with sitting meditation, you can figure out what works best for you. It's a very personal thing. I prefer sitting two short periods - if I can get it together, that is. Once in the morning and again in the afternoon.

Following the Breath

It's the nature of mind to flow on and on like a river, with one thought following another, just as one breath follows another. We are not out to stop that flow. We just want to gently bring our attention away from our thoughts of the past and the future and the *this and the that*, directly into the freshness and timelessness of the present moment. Therefore, the breath, which joins our spirit with our body, and which is *alive*, always fresh and happening right here, right now in the present moment, is the perfect place to put our attention.

So, gently bring your attention to the feeling of your natural breathing rhythm. Feel the air going in and out of your nose, your chest rising and falling. Pay more attention to the outbreath than the inbreath. Just go out and, ahhhh… let go of your thoughts. Go out, and rest your mind in the space before you breathe back in.

Why focus on the outbreath? Because when you get home after a hard days' work you pour yourself a nice, cool drink and put your feet up and you say, "aaaahhhhhhh…..". On the other hand, if you hear terrible news, your breath draws in sharply, "Huh!". So, it's about relaxing the mind.

If you try too hard to pay attention to your breath, your mind will take off into a maze of intense thoughts and emotions. It may be minutes before you're consciously present on the cushion again. Yet, if you relax too much, you'll end up wandering off or even falling asleep. The best approach is 'not too tight, not too loose.' Every time you notice you're thinking, just gently bring your attention back to the breath again and again, without being heavy-handed.

It's important not to judge your thoughts. There are no inherently good or bad thoughts. In the end, they're just thoughts. You don't necessarily have to act on them. They're just thoughts. Let them go. As soon as you realize, "oh, I'm thinking about – whatever – what happened at work yesterday, what needs to be done tomorrow, how to resolve an upsetting conflict between the kids, what's for dinner, politics, world peace," *whatever,* you can gently acknowledge that it's just a thought, not nearly as weighty as it may seem. Just let it go, whatever it is, and bring your attention back to the present.

Ring the Gong to End

Ring the gong once to end, trying not to talk or
move until the sound has completely disappeared. Rest
in the peaceful moment you've created.

Enjoy your coffee, tea or hot chocolate together
before everyone has to get going and the speed slowly
begins to build all over again.

Obstacles to Meditation

One of the greatest obstacles to getting around to
meditating is simply not being able to find the time –
getting sucked into all the other seemingly important
things we feel we must do. Establishing a definite time
frees you from having to plan for it from day to day. It
just becomes a good habit. You don't have to stop and
ask your self, should I practice today? If you think about
it, you wouldn't ask yourself, should I brush my teeth
today? And then decide you don't have the time.
Otherwise your teeth would rot and fall out of your
head! In the same way, if you don't find time to
practice, your naturally peace of mind gets tangled up in
knots. Depression, frustration, anxiety and an
insensitive kind of neurotic speed can slowly build,
subtly changing the way you move through space, the

way you communicate, your ability to properly listen and hear others, and of course, changing the way you feel.

Regular Practice

The best support for regular and consistent meditation practice is that we enjoy doing it. It has become like drinking water. It's refreshing and good in a very down to earth way. It settles any emotional distress or restless energy that might be bothering us and allows us to rest our mind in a joyful state.

If you've ever had the opportunity to watch a great meditator in action, such as the Dalai Lama, or Mahatma Ghandi, you'll notice that even if they're incredibly busy politicians, teachers and world travelers, they're happy. They radiate joy and peace from every pore of their being. It's not because life is less stressful for them. It's simply the cumulative effect of pacifying, stabilizing and strengthening their minds by meditating every day for years and years.

◎

Chapter Five
The Four Main Points of Meditation
An Overview

1. Find a quiet place to sit on the floor in the sacred space you've set up. Sit on a pillow like Geronimo or the Buddha: Cross-legged, with a straight, not rigid back. Gaze softly down at the ground about six feet ahead feet in front (for adults) and two or three feet ahead (for children). Keep your eyes open to remain fully present in the here and now. Keep your gaze unfocused.

2. Ring a gong, a bell, or even a metal mixing bowl(struck with a pencil eraser) to start.

3.   Breathe naturally, not in an affected manner.
Just relax and let your natural breath flow. Feel the cool air coming into your nose and the warmed up air going

out of your nose. Feel your chest rise and fall. If it helps
you to concentrate, count your breaths – one in, two out,
three in...Watch your thoughts and feelings settle down
as you sit still. Every time you start thinking, thinking,
thinking; remember to let go of the thoughts, no matter
how important they might seem. Come back to the
sensation of the air going in and out, in and out.

4. Ring the gong to end. Don't move yet. Wait until
you can't hear the gong anymore. Just relax into the
space.

Part II

The Six Strengths

How Meditation Improves Family Relationships

◎

Chapter Six

About the Six Strengths

Peaceful abiding meditation is said to strengthen the mind in six different ways. These six strengths not only lighten, clarify and uplift our own state of mind, they directly affect the way we communicate (through mindful body language, talking and listening), thus improving our relationships with our spouse and children.

As you read through these, you'll notice these six strengths[5] are just ordinary wisdom that we all possess in varying degrees. Anybody reading this will have experienced them. You could find these qualities in any person, from any walk of life in any culture, at any time in history. They are our human birthright.

─────────────────

[5] The six strengths are also known as the six paramitas.

All we're talking about is how meditation brings out and enhances these strengths that we already have, helping even the youngest of us to resolve emotional issues and maintain a healthy relationship with ourselves and each other. Unburdened, we can behave as fully decent human beings.

◎

Chapter Seven

Space Awareness
How being in the present moment tames us

The natural result of keeping our attention on the freshness of the present moment is that we develop a lucid awareness of our environment and the people in it. When we slow down, come back to earth and relax in the simplicity of each moment, our five sense perceptions come more alive and we see things more clearly. We see things as they *are*. This is the clarity of mind we saw demonstrated in the Mind-in-a-Jar Experiment. Like the naturally clean and clear water, it is the original condition of our mind. Meditation simply brings us back to that natural state. When our actions come from the clarity of the present moment the quality of our communication with our spouse and children gets better and better, simply because we're more aware of what we're doing, how we're moving through space, how our words and actions are affecting others, how they're words and actions are affecting us.

With these six strengths - space awareness, generosity, insight, discipline, patience and joyful energy - we're able to avoid the communication pitfalls we didn't see coming before. We manage to connect where we might have failed to before. Fewer feelings are hurt between family members. As we learn to be kinder to ourselves and each other, slowly, almost imperceptibly, hearts soften and minds open. Genuine understanding grows. Mutual trust deepens. In this way, meditation nourishes family relationships.

The following five strengths are really just aspects of the first one, awareness. So, they're not something we're *trying* to do, they're something we *notice* we're doing when we're in a state of clear awareness. These are qualities we can cultivate through meditation.

◎

Chapter Eight

Unconditional Generosity

Inviting open communication

By generosity I'm not talking about the conventional notion of giving and giving. What I mean here is the generosity of inviting open communication with your spouse or child in that unconditionally open and lucid space we just talked about. That is a hugely amazing gesture to make, if you think about it. Really inviting open communication without pre-judgement, without concept, without rushing, without our own needs getting in the way, without our own agenda interfering. So it's a selfless kind of generosity we're practicing. We're willing to be unconditionally with this person on the spot, inviting open discussion of any kind. It doesn't matter if it's our husband, our wife, our rebellious teenage son or our innocent newborn baby daughter; we simply open up without agenda and spontaneously give whatever the situation requires. That's real generosity.

Taking the time to give our undivided attention when it's truly called for invites authentic communication. There are no longer any hidden corners or sub-levels of communication going on. So many parents wonder why their older children or teenagers don't communicate with them as openly as they once did. In my experience, inviting open communication *unconditionally* was and is always the key to regaining that original openness and trust.

For some of us, it might be hard to admit that sometimes all our children or spouse need are to be left alone, but we can generously give that, too. We give whatever the situation requires, without hesitation.

But seeing precisely what truly is needed in any given situation isn't always that easy. Sometimes we don't know what they really want. How many times have we found ourselves guessing at what we *think* our spouse or children need? How can we get beyond blindly taking a stab in the dark and hoping for the best? For that, we need to be more adept at reading the situation accurately, and not just according to some ideas we've cooked up in our minds. For that, we need the piercing power of real insight, which only arises in the freshness of the present moment.

◎

Chapter Nine
Piercing Insight
Seeing what is

When you're truly focused on the present
moment, paying close attention to your world, you see
things that you ordinarily might not notice. You see the
way your spouse or child is carrying himself, the way he
moves, the way he makes eye contact – or avoids it. You
can read their body language in a more subtle way than
you could before. And you can *feel* things you couldn't
feel before. You can sense a whole range between good
moods and rotten moods that you may simply have
been too preoccupied to notice before. You can sense
subtle levels of delight, warmth, openness and curiosity;
or coldness, indifference, deception and cruelty – all of
these areas can benefit from your loving appreciation
and attention. You know more about the situation at

hand; therefore, you're able to communicate better, simply because you're more informed.

Some people might think it sounds as if we're becoming too sensitive, hypersensitive, paranoid even. But because this insight arises from the naturally compassionate ground of space awareness, it's experienced as relaxed, wide open and spacious at the same time that it's undeniably sharp and clarifying.

Here's a very ordinary example. One day, unbeknownst to me, my six-year-old daughter Tessa's best friend didn't show up for school. When she asked the teacher if her friend Cassidy was sick, the teacher said she had moved away. There had been some family crisis and somehow, in all the bustle, no one ever told Tessa. Did she share her heartbreaking news with me? No. It didn't even occur to her. So, I picked the kids up from school and poor Tessa, who was normally sweet and easy going, raged at everyone in the car. She got mad at her baby sister, Kelly, for slobbering on her in the backseat. She got mad at her brother, Gregory, for looking at her the wrong way. We got home and I made hot chocolate for everyone, and I got it for shorting her a mini-marshmallow. I mean, how could she have even noticed? Was she actually *counting* mini marshmallows? Okay, I said to myself, something's obviously up with Tessa, but I don't have time to deal with it right now. We have to pile back in the car to get something up for dinner... and I promised Hector his favorite dinner.

Luckily, I had actually gotten around to meditating for a half-hour that morning and was feeling pretty calm and clear, and, just at that moment I caught a glimpse of Tessa's face out of the corner of my eye. In a flash of insight, I felt such sadness in her. It touched my heart. Had I been my usual speedy self, I probably wouldn't have even noticed. Resisting the impulse to put a band-aid on the situation by giving her a couple more marshmallows, (possibly a more conventional type of generosity) I decided to just stop and take the time to find out about her day. After fifty questions that got me nowhere: "How was your day?" Okay. "Did anything bad happen at school today?" No.) I finally hit on the magic question.

"Did you eat lunch with Cassidy?", I asked. And the whole sad story came tumbling out.

Chapter Ten
On the Spot Discipline
The right discipline arises on the spot

Normally with discipline we have a certain logic
or philosophy we're trying to adhere to which may or
may not be appropriate to the situation at that particular
moment. Perhaps according to my conventional sense
of discipline I might have put my daughter in time out
for snarling at everybody, and I was tempted to do just
that, but it really wouldn't have gotten to the root of the
problem. I could have erred in the opposite direction by
taking Tessa aside and quietly, solemnly asking her
what the problem was. Like a six-year-old would be
able to articulate all that!

Somehow, in that particular moment, though, it
seemed more appropriate to discipline *myself.* For
someone as speedy as I am, it took real discipline to

force myself to stop, give up my agenda to get to the store in time to get Hectors' favorite dinner on the table at a reasonable hour, and just surrender to the situation at hand. This is insight and discipline arising together. First you see what needs to be done, then you decide to do it – not according to some philosophy you learned somewhere along the way, but according to the messages you're getting in the present moment. So, I had to drop my agenda, choosing to rely on the first two strengths, generosity and insight. I just had to open up and see what the situation required at that particular moment, in that particular time. It had nothing to do with proper ideas of discipline or dinner schedules or shopping or anything else for that matter.

Now, that didn't mean that Tessa was off the hook. Even though she was only six years old and was struggling with a pretty tough transition, we have a rule in our house that everyone is expected to treat each other with respect. So once we'd all comforted her and it became obvious she was *still* grumpy a half-hour later, I suggested she might want to play alone in her room until she was ready to stop snapping at us.

A pretty mundane example, I know. But, I chose that example precisely for its ordinary aspect. These strengths aren't about some exotic wisdom. It's just about humbly improving the quality of ordinary communication with our loved ones. Plain and simple.

◎

Chapter Eleven
Peaceful Patience
Genuine patience brings peace

Sometimes we're so ruled by the clock that it doesn't even occur to us to take time to care for ourselves properly. In our rush to accomplish more and more, we end up eating bad, cheap food on the run; we skip exercise, and we don't get enough rest. There isn't very much self-love in this lifestyle. If we're lucky, we *might* reward ourselves with a treat at the end of a whole week of pushing ourselves.

On the other hand, if we've been meditating, we're more likely to feel a sense of timelessness from moment to moment. We are so thoroughly rooted in the present that we feel freed from the constraints of our schedules. That doesn't mean that we become irresponsible about doing what we need to do, getting to where we need to go on time. We're so afraid we'll become mindless idiots if we loosen our grip even a little bit. But, that's not going to happen. It just means that we feel a sense of 'forever' within each moment, which is tremendously liberating. Honestly, even when we're under a lot of pressure, we don't have to get stressed out about it. It's a relief to allow this feeling of peace, to be open to experiencing the timelessness of each moment. We might be letting go of a bigger burden than we realize.

Interestingly, very young children are already in this state of mind. That's why they're so happy. And that's why meditation is so much easier for kids than for adults. It's not a big leap for them. No big deal. But in this go- go- go- go- go society, the older our children get, the more we have them rushing around. They're constantly dashing to get to school on time, to make the bus, to get to soccer practice, a play date, or piano lessons. On top of that, they're often stressing over homework, disharmony at home, problems with school relationships…you name it. So a peaceful sense of timelessness can help our children just as much as it benefits us. It allows *them* to act calmly, too. Both

parents and children develop that spacious stillness
within which makes the split second difference between
a rash decision and a wise one. A sense of peace from
moment to moment makes us kinder, gentler, more
patient husbands, wives, parents, children and friends;
whereas a sense of rush-rush-rushing makes us irritable,
impatient, insensitive, frustrated, and more easily
angered.

◎

Chapter Twelve

Joyful Energy

The present moment is a wellspring of fresh energy.

As I said earlier, meditation activates the left prefrontal lobe, where positive feelings are generated. Perhaps that's because we're able to tune into the joyful energy that naturally exists in our world. Inherent within every situation, even the most challenging ones, joyful energy perpetually arises in the minds of people who meditate regularly.

Young children demonstrate this truth. Have you ever seen the famous photograph of a little boy with tears streaming down his cheeks and a big fat smile on his face? That is the perfect illustration of being open to the joy of the present moment.

When you aren't burdened with the emotional baggage from what happened a few minutes ago, or for that matter the emotional baggage you inherited from your parents a long time ago, a joyful energy gently arises. (Of course, a little therapy might help, too!)

This uplifting energy can make even the most challenging situations seem workable. Even if something terrible happens - a serious illness strikes the family, or your teenager has gotten in with the wrong crowd and is experimenting with drugs - or you suddenly realize they needed therapy after all for the divorce they apparently never got over - even in these challenging times - this naturally exuberant energy can bubble up. During hard times, it can be experienced as a great wind of confidence that empowers you, making you feel quite capable of working with even the darkest circumstances through to the end. Somehow you know, no matter what it takes, your commitment is complete and you will sail through absolutely. Thanks to your meditative awareness, your insight and generosity, your discipline and patience, your calm and stable mind, you *know* you have what it takes to make it through. Whereas if you're not rooted in the present moment, you could end up caught in the endless maze of your thoughts and emotions, feeling overwhelmed, angry, depressed, confused and depleted. You may find yourself just pushing ahead and saying, "Oh this is so hard. How can I deal with this?"

The blessing of meditation is that it cuts through the heaviness of confusion, helping you and your children to tap into this buoyant energy within the simplicity of each and every moment.

This same energy can be incredibly delightful in happier times where you aren't struggling with a challenging situation. It can be a fresh wind of delight in the day to day communication between your spouse and your children, bringing good humor, a light touch, and a cheerful, positive attitude to everyday life.

Interestingly, if you tried to pinpoint exactly where this vibrant energy comes from, you wouldn't be able to. It seems to arise spontaneously from nowhere. In truth, it's just the natural buoyancy we feel when our energy hasn't been consumed by cluttering up our minds with the entirely unnecessary mental and emotional baggage we talked about earlier. You might think, "I don't waste that much energy with thinking and stressing over things." But as regular meditation makes you more aware of your daily mental activities, you might be surprised to realize just *how much* of your energy gets burned up, tied up in knots, or flattened out as you go about your day to day busy-ness.

◉

Chapter Thirteen

Warrior in the World

*How the six strengths help children and parents cope with
the everyday stresses they face out in the world*

A spiritual warrior in the world is one who,
thanks to their meditative awareness, is sure of their
own ground. Their hearts are naturally open because
knowing their own minds, knowing who they are and
how they feel about things, has given them confidence,
so they don't have to shut down or behave defensively.
Being self-aware and sure of their own ground, they
aren't afraid to walk into any situation with openness.
They're not afraid to stand up for their beliefs, to do the
right thing, to reach out to a friend or sibling in need,
because they're comfortable in their own skin. For those
who practice the six strengths, being a noble-hearted

warrior in the world isn't just some ideal, it's simply the way things naturally unfold.

As caring spouses and parents, we naturally want all family members to be able to face life's everyday challenges with intelligent minds and noble hearts, with clarity and loving-kindness. But the stress our children are under in this neurotic society we live in is more than children have faced in the history of mankind. It makes it so hard for them. They're up against so much. If even so-called minor challenges - like having their best friend move away or being bullied at school can create such upheaval for children, just think what divorce, verbal and emotional abuse, academic pressure, blended families, peer pressure, school gangs and cliques and encountering smoking and drugs can do.

As we know, being able to use our internal resources, and our emotional intelligence, is difficult if we're not in the habit of checking in with ourselves. This may be the number one benefit of regular meditation for the entire family. Most of us are going flat out, kids and parents. We never have the chance to check in with ourselves, to simply be with ourselves, to settle down with ourselves. Even if we're sitting down,

it's usually to busy ourselves with something –
watching TV, eating, reading, doing homework, e-
mailing, surfing the web, talking on the phone. We
never just stop and *be*. As a result reacting wisely when
life suddenly throws you an unexpected curveball can
be difficult. It might be easier to react impulsively,
according to habit, or to just go along with whatever our
peers are doing or saying. But if we're in the daily habit
of stopping and being with ourselves, we'll
automatically check back in and see how we *really* feel
about what's going on.

    Armed with the six strengths, we won't be afraid
to be a warrior in the world – one who isn't crippled by
the weight of old emotional baggage, who walks on this
earth gently, who greets each experience with dignity,
an open heart, and a curious mind.

◎

Epilogue
Creating Peace in the Heart of your Home

Can you imagine what it would be like for your family to gather each morning to practice being peaceful together? Can you imagine what it would be like for your entire family to carry that peaceful experience with them throughout the day?

Instead of waiting for a crisis, like we did, why not jump in and give family meditation a try? Experiment and see for yourself if practicing being peaceful together for ten minutes a day over a three-month period makes your family feel closer, saner and all together happier.

If we can pull it together to brush our teeth everyday, eat nutritional foods and get a good night's sleep, perhaps it's not such a big deal to add a little mental hygiene to our routine as well. Ten minutes a day is all you need to cultivate a peaceful place in the heart of your family.

Questions and Answers

These discussions are from talks given by Hector and Kerry MacLean at Shambhala Mountain Center and Boulder Shambhala Center, from 1996 through 2004: Parenting as Path, Beginning Family Meditation, The Six Paramitas of Parenting, The Eight-Year-Olds' Rites of Passage.

Question: It all sounds great, but I can't help feeling funny about making my children meditate. It reminds me of some bad memories I have of have of my dad making us go to church every Sunday.

Answer: Yeah, I had the same experience. But, we need to be careful not to confuse meditation with religion. Meditation is simply an exercise that can complement any religious practice - or it can stand on it's own. I think in this society our view of meditation is somehow skewed, because it's associated with different religious practices. But meditation in itself can simply be a great way to de-stress, slow down and become fully present. It can *complement* religion, but it isn't a religion in itself.

Q: What about my own personal meditation time? I used to meditate a lot before I had kids.

A: Well, you could continue with whatever you've been doing all along. Or, when the family meditation session is over, you may simply choose to stay on and meditate a while longer. I used to take turns with my girlfriend. We'd bake bread and cinnamon rolls together and take turns sitting in her shrine room while one of us cared for the babies.

Q: I kind of feel like you're discounting the fact that every moment with my child *is* mindfulness practice. Do you really have to sit every single day to develop mindfulness?

A: Well, you're absolutely right. Parenting *is* a form of mindfulness practice. When you have kids you're suddenly forced to pay very close attention all the time. When I had five young ones bouncing around my house,

I used to worry I might lose one! Not only does
parenting force you to be more mindful, but you learn
all about what it *really* means to be patient, selfless,
loving, kind and generous.

But, there's one thing parenting as path doesn't
give you in itself, and that's the wisdom and
spaciousness that comes from being in the present
moment. I mean, it's true that children are a joy to be
with because their hearts are more open and they are
simply more in the present moment than we are; which
forces us to be more in the present moment with *them*,
but that's not quite the same thing as making it a daily
practice to stop our doing, doing, doing and practice just
being - being peaceful together. That makes a powerful
statement. And it does something to us. Our
mindfulness increases tenfold and everything shifts. Our
patience becomes authentic patience. We're no longer
gritting our teeth, *trying* to be patient. We feel the
timelessness of each moment and actually *are* patient.
There's a big difference. With meditation practice our
generosity becomes less about *me* giving *you* something,
and more about surrendering to the present moment,
offering *unconditional* space, *unconditional* attention.

That's a powerful and transformative kind of mindfulness. Now, you feel more relaxed and joyful, which helps everyone you come into contact with to relax and enjoy themselves, as well. And now you're spouse and children truly feel heard - and *seen*, for that matter. It benefits everyone in the family on many different levels.

Q: I'm a Christian. Does meditation conflict with my belief in God?

A: Some of the greatest figures in Christianity meditated, so it shouldn't be a problem. Again, the whole objective of meditation is just to slow us down, and if that slowing down puts us more in touch with our spiritual inspiration, then so much the better! But, it's important not to confuse the two. Meditation is not about beliefs: it's about working with the functioning of our mind and emotions in such a way that we can think and act clearly so that we can avoid inadvertently causing harm to ourselves and others. In that sense, meditation certainly brings you to a spiritual place, but it doesn't *define* what that spiritual place is all about.

That is a very personal matter for each of us to decide for ourselves.

Q: What if my child is too restless to meditate?

A: You shouldn't really expect them to be able to sit for ten whole minutes following their breath until they're about eight years old, although I've seen younger children do it with relative ease. By the time they're nine or ten, though, they really should be able to contain themselves. I've found in my Rites of Passage for Eight-year-olds courses that the kids are quite capable of it; the trick is in getting them to try it without a negative attitude. But, once they're in the habit, even the most restless child can settle into a calming meditative state. Once they've decided they want to try it they just do it without even thinking twice. In general, our children are capable of so much more than we can possibly even begin to imagine.

    If you're talking about younger children, see if you can work with them, encouraging them to sit still and quiet for as long as they can, then let them wander in and out of the sacred space until they're ready to settle down again. They'll keep trying if you keep working with them on it.

For some particularly antsy kids it seems like torture, but they are the ones who stand to benefit the most from meditation, if they can slowly, bit by bit learn to slow down and settle in with themselves. If your child is older and *extremely* restless, it might be more important than ever to teach him or her to slow down. I'm not saying it'll be easy, but in the long run, it'll be a blessing for the child and everyone around them. Don't just assume they'll outgrow it, because maybe they will, maybe they won't, but in the meantime they can make life unnecessarily stressful for themselves and their families. So I strongly encourage you to keep trying to find new ways to work with it. Be patient, don't give up and with enough gentleness and persistence, eventually even the most high-strung child will calm down with meditation over time.

These days we hear a lot about Attention Deficit Disorders of all kinds. The truth is our entire society has attention deficit disorder. Between television, computers and cars, we are constantly entertained, so we never learn to slow down. No wonder our kids can't be still. Some of them are actually insulted you would suggest a thing! So, please, for the whole family's sake, experiment with new approaches to working with them. You might have to get very creative! One way or another it's important to get them to give daily meditation a serious try.

Q: How do you feel about mood altering drugs for adults and children?

A: Now that studies are coming out showing how effective meditation is in stabilizing the mind, curing all kinds of phobias and even improving chronic depression, I'm hoping people will give it a serious try before resorting to drugs that can subtly flatten their personalities and do *who knows what* – perhaps even rob them of their passion for life.

As for children, you know, my youngest daughter, Kelly, was so restless, and she just had so much energy – *too* much energy! We seriously wondered whether the latest drugs would help. She was constantly getting in trouble at school for not paying attention, for literally bouncing off the walls while the teacher talked.

She had a hard time concentrating. She positively vibrated with electricity. We used to make her run around the house twenty times, just to burn off her excess energy. And when that didn't help, we'd make it thirty. Ironically, she ended up being the one who loved meditation the most. She still has way too much energy, but thanks to meditation, she's learned to hold her seat with it. She's learned to harness and use that energy, and as a result she's accomplished an extraordinary amount in her life, and she's only seventeen. So I'm really glad we didn't go the route of experimenting with medications. Who wants to experiment on their child's mind with drugs when meditation is more effective, longer lasting, safer and cheaper?

Q: What if one parent doesn't meditate?

A: I've worked with a couple of families like that. In both cases, the spouse who did meditate invited the other parent to join in just as a test to see how they felt about the family meditation sessions, and in both cases, they enjoyed the family meditation experience and chose to keep it up. Which was a good thing, because it sends a double message to children if you say meditation is important for everyone except the one parent who doesn't feel like meditating. So, obviously it's most beneficial if you can practice together as a whole family.

But be careful. You don't want to be heavy handed about insisting on it. Still, you can warmly invite them to join in and just *try* meditating with you. They just might like it. If you think about it, it's hard to overlook the benefits of practicing being peaceful together as a family. And what we found was that instead of regarding it as yet another thing we had to, we ended up looking forward to the serenity of our family meditation sessions – they were *a pleasure!*

About the Author and her Children's Books

This is Kerry Lee MacLeans' first book for adults. She lives with her husband and two youngest daughters in Boulder, Colorado. She has been meditating for thirty years and is the author and illustrator of the following children's picture books:

- Peaceful Piggy Meditation *New!
- Sophie's Not Afraid!
- Pigs Over Shambhala
  An ABC for young warriors of all ages.
- Pigs Over Boulder
- Pigs Over Colorado

Kerry also co-authored and illustrated these books with Colorado school children:

- Pigs Over Denver
- Pigs Over Colorado Past

Kerry has helped local school children write, illustrate and self-publish their own books, as well:

- Pigs Over Boulder Past *New!
- Pigs Over Louisville

Resources

To find out when Kerry Lee MacLean will be teaching Family Meditative Arts workshops in your area, to order books, to sign up for a certified adult or childrens' meditation instructor (screened), or for kids to learn meditation from interactive peaceful piggies, go to:

www . kerryleemaclean . com

For a variety of high quality adult, teen and children's meditation or meditative arts classes, meditation instructors, and much more in your area go to:

www . shambhala . org

For summer meditation and contemplative arts family camps, children's camps, and much more check out:

www . shambhalamountain . org

For meditation supplies, including colorful children's sized cushions go to:

www . ziji . com

To learn about creating contemplative education programs for children go to:

www . naropa . edu

Recommended books for adults:

Turning the Mind Into an Ally, Sakyong Mipham

Shambhala, the Sacred Path of the Warrior, Chogyam Trungpa

Destructive Emotions, A Scientific Dialogue with the Dalai Lama, Daniel Goleman

Meditation for Optimum Health, Andrew Weil, Md and Jon Cabat-Zinn, Phd

Index